DEVELOPING TEAC

TEACHING MORE
STUDENTS

3
DISCUSSION WITH
MORE STUDENTS

Graham Gibbs

Design Team:
Trevor Habeshaw, David Jaques

Consultant Team:
Gina Wisker, Chris Rust,
David McAndrew, Alan Jenkins,
David Jaques, Trevor Habeshaw,
Graham Gibbs, Bob Farmer,
Diana Eastcott, Sally Brown,
Elizabeth Beaty, David Baume

TEACHING MORE STUDENTS

This publication was originally produced as part of the Polytechnics and Colleges Funding Council funded project entitled 'Teaching More Students'. It involved the training of 3,000 lecturers in workshops at 100 institutions delivered by a team of ten consultants using the following publications as support material:

1   Teaching more students: problems and strategic options
2   Lecturing to more students
3   Discussion with more students
4   Assessing more students
5   Independent learning with more students
6   Supporting more students
    Video: Teaching more students

The project elicited intense interest and Universities and Polytechnics trained an additional 5,500 lecturers using these publications. The impact of this training was evaluated and included instition-wide changes in policy and provision as well as extensive changes in teaching, learning and assessment methods. (Gibbs, 1995)

Gibbs, G. (1995) National-Scale Faculty Development for Teaching Large Classes in W. A. Wright (Ed) *Teaching Improvement Practices*. Bolton: Anker.

Contents

1 Students' experience of discussion groups

"The seminars are a waste of time. Nobody seems to know what we are supposed to be doing, including the tutor who teaches a different course normally. We don't know what the seminar topic means or what we are supposed to have done before so no-one does anything."

"You don't know many people. OK there's the people in the seminar group but there's no way you can get to know everybody. I mean (turns to a student in the group) I've never seen you before."

"It would be nice to ask questions occasionally but the size of the group makes this embarrassing."

"There's too much variance in one module between seminar leaders. With one they might say: 'Right, you've got to have this essay in on this day' and the next one 'OK you're supposed to have it in by this day, but if you don't, you can give it to me tomorrow' or 'That's not relevant to the course, you don't have to do it if you don't want to.'"

"Staff hardly get to know most students and vice versa. Construction of any sort of relationship is therefore impossible."

"The shyer students, who might have the confidence to contribute in small groups, tend to keep quiet in large ones."

"Room allocation for seminars is not always appropriate. A seminar in a large lecture room does not produce a good learning environment."

"In the problem classes it's just like another lecture really. Someone asks a question and off he goes again. I haven't asked a question yet."

"It's really intimidating in the seminars. You've got to stand up in front of all these people you don't really know. There are a couple who seem to revel in it and we just let them get on with it and keep our heads down."

Patterns of discussion in groups

Even in very small discussion groups participants contribute unequally, as illustrated in the graph below. It shows that in a group of five one member of the group made, on average, 43% of the contributions, while the fifth member made only 7% of the contributions (Bligh, 1972).

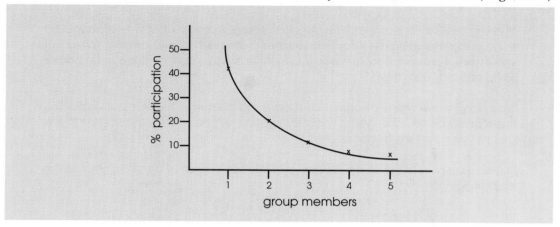

As group size increases, the unequal pattern of contributions becomes more marked, with the one member contributing a great deal more than the rest, and most members speaking very little. In the graph below, for a group of eight, the last five members each made only 3–9% of the contributions.

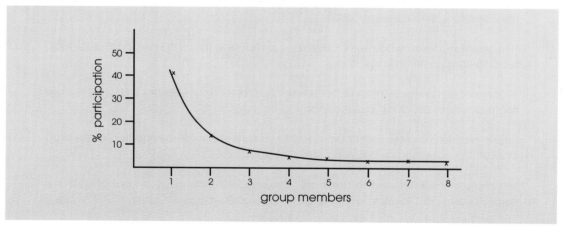

Groups with tutors in them commonly exhibit even more extreme patterns, with the tutor speaking for as much as 80% of the time and most students hardly speaking at all. As seminars increase in size to 12, 20, or even more, it is not difficult to predict the pattern of interaction this produces, with most students hardly involved. As the purpose of seminars is meant to be discussion, such groups clearly do not fulfil their function for most students.

Several changes are necessary if most students are to be actively involved in discussion in larger groups. First, large groups need to be broken down into smaller groups for at least some of the time. Second, the tutor needs to withdraw from discussion for at least some of the time. Third, the influence of dominant students needs to be reduced. The methods described in Section 2 employ these and other strategies.

2 Structures for fostering discussion in larger groups

Conventional discussion groups are unstructured in the sense that at any point anyone can speak while the others listen. There is no structure determining who speaks or what they speak about. This lack of structure provides great freedom to small groups to explore whatever comes up in discussion, and provides the tutor with freedom to pick up on whatever emerges. However, many of the problems encountered in unstructured discussion groups, as they get larger, is caused by this lack of structure. Only one person out of the whole group can speak at any one time, and this becomes more and more like public speaking rather than like a natural intervention into a discussion. In small groups problems of lack of participation and dominance can be handled by adept use of facilitative skills by the tutor. As groups become larger, however, such skills are not enough. The group and the discussion tasks need to be broken up into smaller, more manageable units. This section contains descriptions of 12 such structures:

2.1 Rounds

2.2 Circular interviewing

2.3 Buzz groups, pairs and triads

2.4 Pyramids

2.5 Syndicates

2.6 Fishbowls

2.7 Cross-overs

2.8 Poster tours

2.9 Debates

2.10 Brainstorms

2.11 Line-ups

2.12 Five minutes each way

2.1 Rounds

A round involves each student in the group in turn speaking briefly. It works best if the group sits in a circle and the turn passes round the circle. Rounds work well to start a session as they involve each person speaking once before anyone speaks a second time. This establishes a more balanced pattern of interaction and makes it much more likely that individuals will speak again later.

Rounds at the start of a session might involve themes or questions such as:

"What I've been reading since the last session is ..."

"A question I'd like answered today is ..."

"I hope today's session ..."

Rounds during a session might use themes such as:

"Something we seem not to have really tackled is ..."

"One idea to help us to make faster progress is ..."

"I'd be happy to offer an explanation of ..."

Rounds at the end of a session might use themes such as:

"What I've got out of today is ..."

"Something I still don't really understand is ..."

"What I now intend to read/practise/find out about/work on is ..."

"Next meeting I hope we ..."

Taking your turn in a round can be threatening in a large group, and students unused to rounds should be allowed to "Pass" when it is their turn. However students soon get used to rounds and spontaneously suggest them as ways forward during discussions; for example:

"I think it would be helpful if we all said what we really felt about reading Ibsen. Let's have a quick round on that!"

Rounds need only take 15 seconds per person, though you can suggest much longer and slower rounds if you want to encourage extensive exploratory and reflective talk.

2.2   Circular interviewing

Although rounds succeed in getting everyone to join in, students tend to speak to the tutor rather than to each other and you end up establishing a pattern of interaction as illustrated in diagram (a) below.

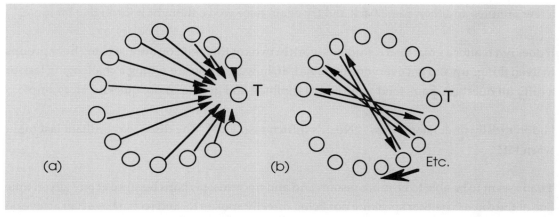

Circular interviewing involves each person interviewing the person opposite about an agreed topic for a moment or two and then both the interviewer and the interviewee roles rotating one place around the group until everyone has taken both roles, as in diagram (b) above.

This pattern has the advantage, over rounds, of everyone both asking and answering questions, and of these interactions happening across the group in every direction rather than only to the tutor. Circular interviewing is very likely to initiate subsequent discussion across the group between students.

Circular interviews can take themes such as:

"Find out what the other person has read which throws light on ..."

"Find out what the other person would really like to be discussing today ..."

"Find out what questions the other person would like answers to today ..."

Circular interviewing takes longer than rounds and can, because students find it engaging, take rather too long if you let it.

2.3   Buzz groups, pairs and triads

Buzz groups are simply small groups of two or three students formed impromptu to discuss a topic for a short period. In a pair it is almost impossible for a student to stay silent and once students have spoken "in private" they are much more likely to speak afterwards "in public" in the whole group. Buzz groups are very useful to get things going. The sound of ten pairs buzzing is quite energising compared with one person speaking in a group of 20. Buzzes can also tune students in to your subject matter and wind up their ideas; for example:

"To start off, let's buzz for five minutes on what your initial reactions were to the readings I set for this week's seminar. Off you go."

They are also useful when a difficult topic or some awkwardness has brought a session to a standstill; for example:

"Well that seems to have stopped us in our tracks! Let's try and tackle that in buzz groups for a few minutes and then come back and try again once we've thought it through a bit more."

It does not matter a great deal if students work in twos or threes if you are just using buzz groups to liven things up and get everyone involved. If, however, you are setting a challenging task or a difficult question, pairs tend to be less disciplined and give up more quickly; for example:

"I don't really understand this." "No, it's difficult isn't it?" "The disco was brilliant last night wasn't it?"

Triads seem to be able to be more resourceful and rigorous, perhaps because at any given time one of the three is neither speaking nor being directly spoken to, and so can have half an eye on the question or task the group is supposed to be working on. Triads will keep at tasks for longer without drifting off the topic.

2.4 Pyramids

Pyramid groups, also known as "snowball" groups, involve students working alone, then in pairs, then in fours or sixes, and finally as a whole group in a plenary. Pyramidding is a very effective way to lead into productive discussion in even a large group, such as 24.

Working alone might involve reading a passage or a case study or beginning to tackle a problem. It gives students a chance to wind some ideas up and have some material to talk about even before they are put in pairs.

In pairs students can risk being very exploratory and tentative in a way which is too exposing in larger groups. This is where ideas develop from seeds into flowering ideas.

In fours or sixes most of the real work gets done. A group this size is ideal for developing both a range of views and full involvement. As ideas will have been tried out already in pairs, students do not feel inhibited about expressing them.

Plenary sessions, involving all the groups of four or six, can take the form of pooling points from each group in turn or open discussion. For groups of up to about 24 this is still worthwhile, though in larger groups plenaries have more of a ritual function. Everyone wants to know a little about what others were discussing, but only a little, and a few people want their chance to say their bit in public, though this may not be especially illuminating to everyone else. Plenaries do, however, allow the tutor to take the discussion to a higher level and to challenge the ideas generated by the students.

The balance between the stages depend on the size of group but might typically involve:

5 minutes   Working individually

15 minutes   Sharing and discussing in pairs

30 minutes   Comparing and debating in fours or sixes

10 minutes   Pooling and gaining an overview in a plenary

Pyramids can become as dull as unstructured sessions if used repeatedly without variation in their structure or the kinds of discussion tasks or questions set at each stage. In pyramids students can move from concrete to abstract, from easy to difficult, from simple to complex, from small, short tasks to larger, longer tasks as they move from working alone to working in fours.

The role of the tutor is to design the instructions for each stage, tell students what to do next and handle the plenary. It is often best to keep out of the fours' discussions and almost always best to keep out of the pairs. Pyramids are so easy to run that you can feel redundant.

2.5 Syndicates

Syndicates are teams of students working in parallel on the same task. They might be designing something, analysing a problem or case, studying a text or artifact, or preparing a proposal or bid. Normally syndicates present the outcomes of their discussions in a plenary session. This is where the whole group discussion comes in. Syndicates tend to be task-orientated teams rather than simply discussion groups and may be in competition with other teams; both these features can increase motivation and involvement. It is possible to have many syndicates working in parallel in the same room: as many as a dozen teams of eight are perfectly manageable. Obviously suitable accommodation is important: a flat-floored room in which furniture can be moved without difficulty is most appropriate.

The tutor's role is to design suitable tasks and to brief the teams clearly. Students may need resources, handouts or advice as they work. The tutor can move from team to team checking that they are making progress on the task. If one empty chair is set up at the blackboard end of each team this makes it easier for the tutor to join the teams without disrupting them too much, and easier for teams to invite the tutor in, as illustrated below.

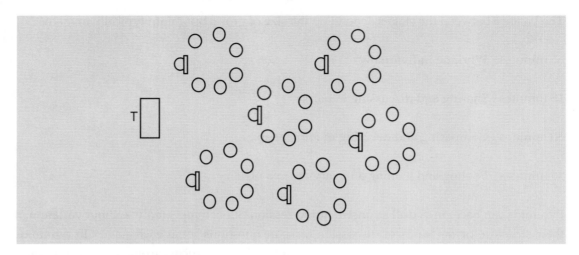

The final stage, in which the teams report on their conclusions, designs or analyses, can be dull, especially if it involves a long sequence of similar and poorly prepared oral reports. It should either be kept short or an alternative technique for pulling together the team work should be tried, such as fishbowls or cross-overs.

2.6   Fishbowls

A fishbowl is a small circle of chairs occupied by students who will have a discussion, surrounded by a larger circle of chairs occupied by the rest of the students who will listen in.

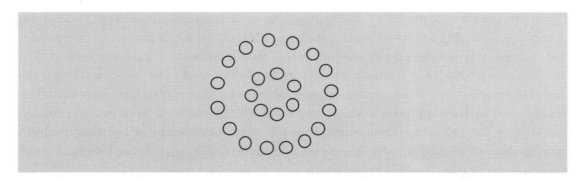

It is most useful when you have quite a large group, perhaps 30 or more, in which a discussion involving the whole group would be desultory, fragmentary and dominated by only a few students. Those students who would have spoken up in the whole group will readily volunteer to go into the fishbowl, and these students will have a more lively and coherent discussion simply because they are close together. The other students would not have joined in anyway and at least have a livelier discussion to listen to.

You can offer a way for those in the outer circle to join in the discussion by simply "tapping out" those in the fishbowl. Anyone from the outer circle may replace anyone in the fishbowl by tapping them on the shoulder; the two swap seats and the new person joins in the fishbowl discussion. Not only does this allow people to join in if they want to, it also allows students to get rid of those they have heard enough of!

Fishbowls can be used to de-brief syndicate work. One representative of each syndicate goes into the fishbowl to discuss what their team got up to.

2.7 Cross-overs

Cross-overs are a way of changing the make up of groups within a larger class. If you have six groups of six working in a room you can re-mix them so that each of the six new groups consists of one member from each of the six old groups, as illustrated in the diagram below.

Cross-overs are useful for sharing ideas across groups and the outcomes of syndicate work. Conventional reporting-back methods rely on one person being rapporteur. Everyone else in the group can then sit back while only the rapporteur takes notes and pays attention. At the reporting-back stage only the rapporteurs are actively involved. With cross-over groups every single student has responsibility for being rapporteur for their group, and all the reporting back occurs in small groups instead of in the whole class. This makes reporting back more interesting and more likely to involve questioning and discussion.

2.8 Poster tours

It helps groups working together on a task, such as syndicates, to use a board or flip-chart. Having to produce a poster of the outcomes of the discussion also focusses attention on a clear goal. Posters can involve a design or proposal, lists of the pros and cons of an approach, or the main features of a case study. De-briefing this syndicate work can then take the form of displaying the posters. This is a process used at academic conferences to share the outcomes of research work, and learning to communicate in poster form is a useful academic skill. Posters can be specially quick and effective means of sharing experimental and laboratory work where different groups have been undertaking different experiments.

Once the posters are displayed, students simply tour them. To make the tour more interactive you can:

• ask one member of each group to stay by their poster to answer questions;

• place blank poster sheets next to each poster for graffiti for students to comment, ask questions and respond to these comments.

2.9 Debates

Debates give structure and focus to discussions and make it more likely that students will join in even when the group is fairly large. Highly organised debates, such as in the example below, may support independent small-group discussion over a number of weeks prior to the large-group event at which the debate takes place. This can be a very effective way to generate productive student discussion which involves very little tutor time. However, tutor time is involved in setting up a debate on this scale: designing the whole exercise, briefing the students and preparing handouts. Unlike conventional seminars they cannot be handled off the top of your head. This example is one of a range of similar processes drawn from a manual on the development of group skills.

"Role Playing Royal Commission" was designed by John Gold and is extracted from A. Jenkins and D. Pepper, *Enhancing Employability and Educational Experience : Developing Communication and Group Work Skills.* Birmingham SCED 1989.

Role Playing Royal Commission

Brief description

The class takes on the form of a Royal Commission. Students are briefed to represent the viewpoints of various interest groups over a period of weeks.

Aims

To develop students' ability to work in groups, research an issue, speak in public and write a report from a particular perspective.

Courses used in

Various courses in urban geography; but suitable for any course where different groups in society will have marked differences about the approach to be adopted to a particular issue.

What the teacher does

Decide upon the issue to be investigated. This approach is particularly suitable for analysing how different interest groups formulate their courses of action on the same issue. Thus it is suited to a wide variety of political or social issues which in the "real world" could be the subject of a Royal Commission or Public Enquiry (see the description of an enquiry into the problems of the inner city). The method can also be used for issues of a more overtly scientific nature, e.g. what are the best forms of sea defence or what are the causes of and solutions to the problems of acid rain?

Decide upon the interest groups to be represented at the enquiry. The number of interest groups will largely depend on the variety of interest groups and opinions on this issue in the "real world" and the number of students for whom you have to find roles. Each interest group should be formed of about two to four people: if a group becomes larger than four, co-ordinating the group can become difficult and some students may play a very marginal role.

Pick one student to chair the Royal Commission. This should not be left to student choice. Much of the success of the exercise depends upon the person playing this role. She needs to be someone liked and respected by her peers but able to act in authority. Of course you (or another member of staff) can choose to play that role, but it then becomes a teacher-centred rather than a student-centred activity.

Divide students into the various interest groups in whatever way you think appropriate. It can be very valuable for students to take on a role with which they are initially not in sympathy. This can enable them to get to grips with a viewpoint they do not readily understand. However, this presents a danger that they will not forcefully or convincingly argue from that position.

The following are extracts from assignment instructions outlining Royal Commission procedures.

Assignment: Royal Commission on the Problems of the Inner City

By decree of Parliament, a Royal Commission has been established to investigate the state of government policy towards the inner city. Its terms of reference are:

to investigate the problems of the inner city, to discover the nature of those problems, their causes and their consequences, and to make recommendations about the priorities that should be adopted in future planning for the inner city.

The Commission has decided to supplement its own readings of documentation and other literature by calling evidence from the following bodies:

The City of Birmingham, the City of Glasgow, the Confederation of British Industry, the Trades Union Congress, the Church of England and the Town and Country Planning Association

You can play either of two roles:

1 represent one of these interest groups both in the form of a written submission (to be written as a group paper) and by speaking and acting on behalf of your interest group in all the class sessions;

2 act as a member of the Commission, whereby you will hear evidence, cross-question your witnesses, sift through the evidence and prepare a joint report.

In either case, 50% of the marks for this assignment are awarded for the written paper supplied by your group and 50% for your own group's performance in the class sessions, i.e. how convincingly you have performed your role. Remember, if you are to represent an interest group satisfactorily, you must be prepared to twist the evidence, lie convincingly and do whatever else is necessary to support your case just as you would if this was a real Commission of Enquiry. The success of any simulation depends on the willingness of all participants to enter into the spirit of the exercise. This criterion will be taken into account in marking the simulation.

You are free to take on any role that you wish, subject to the fact that Parliament, in the shape of your tutor, will be appointing the Chairperson.

TIMETABLE (2-hour session each week)

Week	Tasks
1	Introductory session (Teacher), followed by brief plenary session.
2	Evidence from (1) City of Birmingham, (2) City of Glasgow.
3	Evidence from (1) CBI, (2) TUC.
4	Evidence from (1) C of E, (2) TCPA.
4 - 8	Commission prepares report, which is handed in for duplication and distribution.
9	Beginning of week: pick up copy of report for reading before the last session. Final session Commission presents report, cross-examination of Commission, de-briefing.

Rules for the simulation

1   All working sessions of the simulation are run by the Chair of the Commission. He or she, in conjunction with the other members of the Commission, will direct the proceedings, will retain order, and will ensure that the presenting group gets a fair chance to put across its case and that other participants have an opportunity to cross-question.

2   Oral presentations of evidence ought not to take more than 30 minutes and must not take more than 35 minutes. Clear presentations, using visual or other material to achieve effective communication, will be rewarded.

3   Participants are expected to perform their particular roles at all times during the simulation. Failure to do so will cost marks; equally, success in doing so gains marks.

4   Attendance at the simulation sessions is compulsory.

5   Controversy should never be avoided on the grounds of student solidarity. Indeed, given the fact that the exercise involves groups who in reality are opposed to one another's point of view, one would expect controversy. You are all more likely to score good marks in a heated session in which everyone participates, and the interest group or Commission is put under pressure to explain or defend its views, than in a bland and genteel session that bores the pants off everyone.

6   Under the rules of the simulation, the tutor is present only as an observer and assessor; the tutor is NOT allowed to take any active role in discussions NOR can he or she be called upon to adjudicate on issues. The Chair's word is final on all questions involving the running of the simulation.

2.10   Brainstorms

Brainstorming is a technique for creative problem-solving. It involves a group of up to about 12 in launching ideas, initially without any discussion, elaboration or criticism, and then going back through the list of ideas generated to see which ones are worth pursuing. It is the separation of the creative from the analytic stages which makes brainstorming work. Normally ideas are strangled at birth because of worries that they might be silly or unworkable. The larger the group the more likely it is that students will be reluctant to express half-formed ideas in the context of unstructured discussion.

Brainstorming is an excellent way of getting a discussion group to generate some interesting material they can then work with. It need only take five minutes at the start of a session and can both provide an agenda of possible content for the discussion and establish a light, quick, interesting tone for it. Students can learn to use brainstorming for themselves, and multiple groups within a room can each undertake their own brainstorm without requiring a tutor in each group.

Brainstorming requires some simple ground rules if it is to work. Each group should appoint a scribe, to record the ideas thrown up. These should be recorded on a board or flip-chart so that everyone can see, and not in notes on a pad that only the scribe can see. A clear brief is required; for example:

"The theme for this brainstorm is 'In what ways are Chekhov and Pinter similar?'."

"Let's brainstorm ideas for tackling this management problem."

As group members call out their ideas they should not elaborate, explain themselves or use long sentences. The idea is to say a word or phrase that stands for the idea, which the group can come back to later, and which the scribe can record quickly so as not to hold up the flow of ideas. No-one except the person who calls out the idea need understand what it means at this stage, and even that person need not be clear. There should be no comments, questions or, especially, criticism. This is not a discussion that comes later. Groups new to brainstorming may need to appoint a referee to call out "Foul!" if members break this ground rule.

After ideas have dried up, the group goes back through the list to see what the words mean that the scribe has recorded. At this point many of the ideas will seem to be unproductive but some will stand out as worth working on. The group selects several of these ideas and has an open discussion of them. The pattern and content of this discussion tends to be very different from, and much more productive than, what would have happened without the brainstorm.

2.11   Line-ups

Line-ups involve asking students to come clean on where they stand on a controversial issue by asking them, literally, to stand at a position in a line which represents their views. The tutor's role is to define what the line, the dimension of views, consists of, and to get students up out of their chairs. Such dimensions might be:

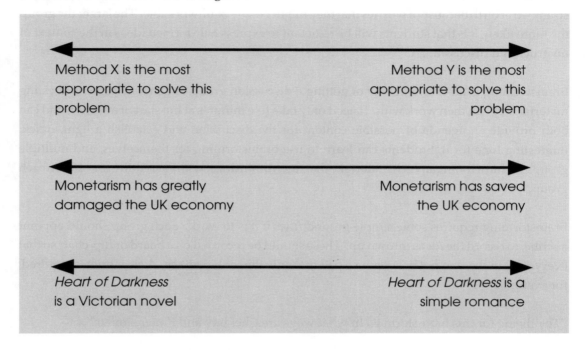

Students will need to talk to those either side of them in the line-up to find out if they are in the right place in the line in relation to others, and this generates a great deal of lively discussion. It is also possible to change aspects of the dimension, introducing new variables, to get students to consider more subtle issues. For example students would probably change their position in the line in response to the following variation on the economics line-up above:

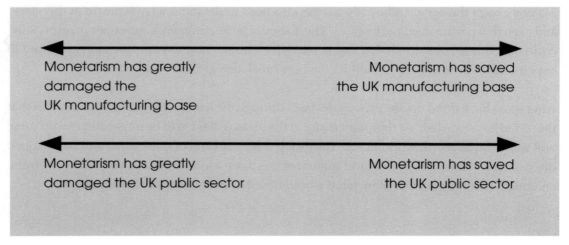

Line-ups can provide students with plenty of issues to discuss when they sit down again and need take only a couple of minutes to run. They take little or no preparation and can be run even with very large groups.

2.12   Five minutes each way

Many of the methods described above involve little or no tutor involvement in a discussion, and tutors might worry about the degree of intellectual rigour in the discussion that will take place. Indeed in normal social interaction people collude to avoid difficulties and complexities, especially where personal issues or strongly held or tentative views are involved. One method, which has the effect of pushing independent pairs to follow an argument a bit further and confront the limits of their understanding, is to ask students to take turns in thinking through a topic out loud, without interruption. It is derived from co-counselling and involves each person taking turns and having an equal amount of time (for example, five minutes each way) and the listener doing just that, simply listening. The only role for the listener is to pay attention and to bring the speaker back to the topic if they drift off. For example, if the topic was "Is *Heart of Darkness* a Victorian novel?" the listener would not speak except to say "So is *Heart of Darkness* a Victorian novel?". It is crucial that the listener does not take pity on a struggling or silent speaker and bale them out. Five minutes each way can be very hard work and students find it very challenging.

Themes for this kind of process could be:

"Problems I'm having with this kind of calculation".

"Aspects of the Law of Tort which I need to clarify".

"Behaviourism in relation to my own experience of learning".

"How I could go about this essay".

"Five minutes each way" exercises can be used at the start of sessions to get students going, during sessions to introduce a bit of reflection and involve everyone, or at the end to summarise learning or set action plans.

The 12 methods described above can be mixed within sessions and should be varied from week to week. When introducing new methods, take care to explain to students why you are doing it and what benefits you expect. Take an experimental approach ("Let's try something new to see if it helps to tackle the problem of ...") and review the effectiveness of methods with students ("Was that useful? Would you like to try using that kind of method again?"). Students are then much more likely to co-operate with you and see the success of the session as a joint venture rather than see the exercises as daft and trivial games foisted on them by an eccentric tutor.

3 Dealing with difficult incidents in larger groups

However skilful you are and whatever techniques you use you are likely to run into difficult situations in large discussion groups. Challenges, being more "public", can be more threatening, and because there are more students it is harder to spot these coming and deal with them quietly. This exercise offers an opportunity to develop strategies to cope with these difficult incidents. While many of these incidents are not unique to large groups, they are more likely to occur in large groups and are more difficult to avoid and to tackle.

3.1 Problem incidents

For each problem incident which is an issue for you, make notes on how you might deal with it. Start off by identifying two problem incidents of your own which you would like to work on.

Problem incident	How you could deal with it
1 The whole group is silent and unresponsive.	
2 Individuals are silent and unresponsive.	
3 Sub-groups start forming with private conversations.	
4 The group becomes too deferential towards the tutor.	

Problem incident	How you could deal with it
5 Discussion goes off the point and becomes irrelevant.	
6 A distraction occurs (such as two students arriving late).	
7 Students have not done the preparation, or do not know what they should have done.	
8 Members do not listen to each other, and discussion does not build on previous contributions.	
9 Students do not answer when you ask a question.	
10 Two students are very dominant and hog the discussion.	
11 Students complain about the seminar and the way you are handling it.	
12 Students reject the seminar discussion process and demand answers.	
13 The group picks on one student in an aggressive way.	
14 Discussion focuses on one corner of the group and the rest stop joining in.	

3.2 Dealing with problem incidents

Below are some suggestions for dealing with the incidents listed above. They fall into three broad strategic types:

1 Don't start from here

This is where the problem has occurred because appropriate steps have not been taken at an earlier stage. For example, the students may not have been introduced to each other, the purpose of the seminar may not have been made clear, the preparation that was required may have been unclear or impossible, or the social ground rules of the session may not have been established appropriately. Until these prerequisites are sorted out you may be repeatedly fire-fighting in the seminar and the incident will keep recurring. An example of paying attention to the initial setting up of seminar groups up so that problems are less likely to occur later can be found in Section 5.

2 Use structures

Unstructured large group discussions are almost bound to fail. Many incidents are an inevitable consequence of lack of structure. Both the process and the content need to be structured. Suggestions for structures can be found in Section 2.

3 Make leadership interventions

These are the really skilful things experienced tutors learn to say and do which subtly redirect groups, defuse situations, bring in quiet students and so on. In larger groups you may need to be less subtle and more assertive about your interventions, and skills you have developed in small groups may not be as effective. You may need to be a great deal more explicit about what you are doing and what behaviour you are expecting and you may need the co-operation of the group to tackle the problem.

For example, instead of using body language or gestures to shut one student out and bring in another, you may need to say :

"I've noticed that some of you have done most of the talking while others have had little opportunity to join in. I'd like everyone to do whatever they can to produce a more balanced pattern of discussion. This may mean keeping a little quieter or asking others to join in by asking them questions."

You may only need to resort to strong leadership interventions if you have paid attention to prerequisites and if you persist with large unstructured discussion groups.

Possible solutions to problem incidents

1 The whole group is silent and unresponsive
Use rounds, buzz groups or pyramids to get people talking and energised. Ask "What is going on?" Ask fours to discuss what could be done to make the group more lively and involving and then pool suggestions.

2   Individuals are silent and unresponsive
Use open, exploratory questions. Invite individuals in: "I'd like to hear what Chris thinks about this." Use buzz groups.

3   Sub-groups start forming with private conversations
Break them up with sub-group tasks. Ask "What is going on?". Self- disclosure: "I find it hard to lead a group where ..."

4   The group becomes too deferential towards the tutor
Stay silent, throw questions back, open questions to the whole group. Negotiate decisions about what to do instead of making decisions unilaterally.

5   Discussion goes off the point and becomes irrelevant
Set clear themes or an agenda. Keep a visual summary of the topics discussed for everyone to see. Say; "I'm wondering how this relates to today's topic." Seek agreement on what should and should not be discussed.

6   A distraction occurs (such as two students arriving late)
Establish group ground rules about behaviour such as late arrivals. Give attention to the distraction.

7   Students have not done the preparation
Clarify preparation requirements, making them realistic. Share what preparation has been undertaken at the start of each session. Consider a contract with them in which you run the seminar if they do the preparation, but not otherwise.

8   Members do not listen to each other
Point out what is happening. Establish ground rules about behaviour. Run a listening exercise.

9   Students do not answer when you ask a question
Use open questions, leave plenty of time. Use buzz groups.

10 Two students are very dominant
Use hand signals, gestures and body language. Support and bring in others. Give the dominant students roles to keep them busy (such as note-taker).Use structures which take away their audience.

11 Students complain about the seminar and the way you are handling it
Ask for constructive suggestions. Ask students who are being negative to turn their comments into positive suggestions. Ask for written suggestions at the end of the session. Agree to meet a small group afterwards.

12 Students reject the seminar discussion process and demand answers
Explain the function of seminars. Explain the demands of the assessment system. Discuss their anxieties.

13 The group picks on one student in an aggressive way
Establish ground rules. Ask "What is going on?". Break up the group using structures.

14 Discussion focuses on one corner of the group and the rest stop joining in
Use structures. Point out to the group what is happening. Check the layout of the room.

4   Using seminar guides to support multiple discussion groups

This section concerns the design and use of printed guides to seminars as a way of coping with the organisational complexity and learning difficulties for students of having many parallel seminars, often run by different tutors.

4.1   Tutor guides

When there are multiple seminar groups it is usual to employ a team of lecturers to help out rather than have one lecturer run perhaps a dozen or more identical seminars each week. We know of courses which have as many as 25 parallel seminar groups for each of five parallel courses, which means there are 125 seminars a week to find tutors for! Inevitably some of those brought in will have only a tenuous involvement in the course. They may be part-time or have unrelated subject specialisms. They will not have time to attend all the lectures to tune in to what students are likely to be studying each week and they will not know the students at all well. They may have no contact with the students other than in the seminars. They may not have anything to do with setting or marking assignments or exams. Consistency of standards and coverage and the quality of briefing of students is likely to suffer. Seminars can become poorly related to the lectures and to the rest of the course. They can become aimless and very difficult to tutor.

In these circumstances it is very helpful to have a seminar guide for the tutors. Such a guide should contain all the information given to students (see below) and additional information to help tutors to run the seminars; for example:

- Suggestions for exercises or discussion formats for each seminar. The seminar group is likely to be large and if students are not well prepared an unstructured discussion is unlikely to work well. These suggestions can take the kinds of ideas in this section and apply them to specific topics.

- Handout material for students to read, discuss and work on during the seminar.

- Suggestions on advice to students for preparation for the next seminar.

- Reminders about what is happening in other parts of the course (for example, visiting speakers or field trips).

- Suggestions for study-skills exercises, complete with instructions and materials, which may be run if the group appears to need to work on their reading skills, essay-writing skills, organisation of time, etc. Ideas for such exercises can be found in Habeshaw *et al.* (1989).

- Information about assessment, including regulations, deadlines, when to collect work to be marked, about the exam and about marking criteria.

- Information about assessment of seminar presentations, should this be a responsibility of the tutor.

If you are unsure what to include in a tutor guide, ask your tutors what they would like to know about and what support they would like. Whenever possible write this information and advice down so that it can act as a reminder to tutors and can be used to brief new tutors who are brought in as replacements or to cope with unexpected extra seminar groups.

4.2 Student guides

When you have multiple seminar groups the seminars are likely to be taken by a range of tutors not otherwise connected with the course. Briefing of the students for the next seminar is often weak and preparation is consequently poor. Contact with tutors outside seminars is unlikely and students lack the opportunity to clarify what they are supposed to read or do between seminars. The focus of the seminar is likely to be less clear and everyone may be uncertain about what should be achieved.

In such circumstances it can make a great deal of difference to provide a detailed guide to the seminars. If you want students to lead their own seminar groups or if you want to run multiple groups in parallel single-handed (see Section 5) then seminar guides can be particularly useful.

Seminar guides which list the topics, seminar groups, dates and key readings for each topic are not uncommon, but they are often insufficiently detailed to provide the necessary guidance for students in very large classes. Seminar guides can also contain:

- Outlines of the topics, making it clear why they have been chosen and how they fit into the course. A conceptual overview of the pattern of seminars is particularly useful as many of the tutors will not have this overview.

- Objectives for each seminar, stating what learning outcomes should be aimed at.

- Annotated bibliographies for each seminar, providing more detailed guidance concerning what students could hope to gain from each of the books, pointing out their strengths and weaknesses, theoretical stance, usefulness for particular issues and so on.

- Alternative readings. In large classes students' most frequent experience is finding that the recommended books are already on loan from the library. A wider range of sources should be suggested.

- Special readings for seminar participants. It is unreasonable to suggest that 500 seminar participants all read a particular journal article in the same week when there will already be 25 or so seminar presenters chasing the same material. You will need to have a short list of easily accessible reading for participants, perhaps in a set book. It is more effective to be realistically modest in your expectations than to have all the participants except the presenter completely ignorant about the topic.

- Discussion questions to help focus reading and to prime students as to what could be discussed in the seminar.

- Specially written overviews of the topics of perhaps one to two pages per topic. These can provide the kind of framework which neither the readings nor many of the tutors could give.

- A full timetable of seminars so that students can pick up other seminar groups if they have timetable clashes or other problems.

- A full list of names so that students can contact others in their seminar group or find friends in other groups. It is easy to become anonymous when you are one student in 20 in one of 25 parallel seminar groups.

- Explanations of assessment and peer-assessment mechanisms and criteria when seminar presentations or involvement in seminar groups are assessed.

- Explanations of any special discussion formats used (see Section 2).

- Exhortations to take the seminars seriously, backed up, if possible, by feedback from last year's students on how useful they found them.

- Advice on how to prepare for seminars, including library information and advice on reading and note-taking.

- Advice on how to take part productively in seminars, including advice on how to avoid being difficult and on how to deal with others who are being difficult. This can include checklists to help students to review the way they run their own seminars.

- Advice on how to (and how not to) give seminar presentations, together with an offer of brief tutorial support before such presentations.

5   Setting up and supporting independent discussion groups

Using student and tutor guides (see Section 4) will help to solve the organisational and teaching problems of parallel seminar groups but you will still need to find the tutors to lead all the seminars. One solution to this staffing problem is to set up independent, tutor-less groups. Students are perfectly capable of having productive discussion without a tutor being present, but they are unlikely to do so without help in setting up the independent groups, and supporting them once they are established. There are potential gains and losses for both tutors and students of having independent discussion groups, and decisions about whether to introduce them, and how to set them up and support them, should be based on a strong sense of what the potential losses might be, and how to minimise these. Use the table below to analyse the situation.

Gains and losses with independent tutor-less discussion			
	Potential **Gains**	Potential **Losses**	How to maximise the gains and minimise the losses
for the **Tutor**			
for the **Students**			

Below are two case studies of courses where care was taken to establish effective independent groups. In the first a training day was put aside to develop students' tutorial groups and seminar presentation skills. In the second the seminars were assessed by the students themselves and the rigour within the groups came from this peer-assessment.

5.1 Case study 1: Setting up independent first-year seminars in Italian

This case study involved the first year of an Italian course in which students had weekly seminars for the historical component. Throughout the year the students would take turns to give seminar presentations. In the past the seminars had gone very badly, with little interest or preparation from anyone other than the seminar presenter, poor-quality presentations and a very unconducive atmosphere in the groups.

Eight parallel independent seminar groups of eight were set up for a class of 64 students. A training day was run during the students' induction week, to help the groups to form, discuss how they wanted to operate, and practise giving seminars. The programme for this day is reproduced below. It was run by one tutor who could easily have handled more parallel groups and more students. Second- and third-year students were invited to share their experience of dreadful seminars in the negative brainstorm exercise.

In the practice seminars students chose their own topics (such as "Rock bands in the 70s") and prepared overhead transparencies, flip-chart posters and handouts. They gave the seminars as pairs to reduce the stress involved and increase co-operation.

The handouts "Improving Seminar Presentations" and "Involving Students in Discussion" were used in briefing students about how to run their seminars. The practice seminars all took place in one large room, and with no involvement whatsoever on the part of the tutor. The students' first experience of seminars in higher education was therefore of independent groups where the groups themselves had total responsibility for their own operation. The handout: "Seminar Presentation Feedback Form" was used by the groups to give feedback to the seminar presenters.

The day ended with each student making a statement about what they had learnt about seminars or about how they would make their seminar groups more pleasant and effective. Each seminar group formulated plans for monitoring their own performance as a group.

Seminar Group Training Session

Aims

- To introduce students to each other.
- To establish effective seminar groups.
- To develop effective seminar group working practices.
- To develop seminar presentation skills.
- To establish a method for giving feedback to seminar presenters to improve their presentations.

Programme

10.00 Introduction

10.10 Team formation

Establishment of seminar groups of eight and a team-building exercise in which students had 30 minutes in which to turn themselves from an anonymous cluster into a functioning team.

10.40 Doing it wrong ...

A negative brainstorm and discussion of how to make tutorials dreadful, helped by second and third-year students, followed by a display of posters.

11.00 Coffee

11.20 Doing it right...Ground rules

Groups discuss the opposite of how to make seminars dreadful in order to establish the ground rules they wish to work to. Each group displays and signs their own set of ground rules on a poster.

12.00 Effective presentations and discussions

A very brief presentation based on a handout

12.20 Preparation for seminars in the afternoon

Each pair in the seminar groups of eight will have the chance to give a 20 minute seminar: ten minutes, presentation, and ten minutes, discussion, followed by five minutes, feedback. The pairs have until 2.20 to prepare.

2.20 Practice seminars
2.20   1st seminar pair
2.45   2nd seminar pair
3.10   3rd seminar pair
3.35   4th seminar pair

4.00 Tea

4.20 Closing exercise

Each person in turn completes one of the following the sentences:
"Something I'm going to do to make my seminar group work well is ..."
"How I feel about being in my seminar group is ..."
"Something we have learnt as a group is ..."

4.30 Close

Improving Seminar Presentations

These guidelines identify the common mistakes students make in seminar presentations and suggest how to avoid them.

1 Forgetting there is an audience
A presentation does not only involve you speaking, it also involves your audience listening. Why should your audience bother listening to what you have to say? You have to interest them at the start and find ways of making them listen. Think about what might intrigue them, puzzle them, contradict their expectations, be controversial or entertaining. Think about what they already know and how they could relate that to what you have to offer. Think about your audience, not just about your material.

2 Including too much content
Inexperienced presenters almost always have too much material to present and rush through it, overburdening their audience and still taking too long. 15 minutes is the limit on most people's concentration even when the presentation is riveting. Cut down your content and slow down on your rate of presentation. If you are worried about running out of materials either time yourself (presenting at an even pace into a mirror), or give yourself time-fillers such as extra examples, something for the audience to read, or questions for the audience to answer and discuss part-way through your presentation.

3 Lack of direction
It is difficult for an audience to listen to you for long if they don't know where you are going with your talk, or why. You need to explain, at the start, what your audience are in for and where you will take them. It isn't much help just saying: *"Today is about X."* You need to explain how you will tackle X and what you will spend time on; for example: *"My presentation today is about X. What interests me about this is the question of Y. I'd like to look at this question in three ways, A, B and C, and illustrate these with examples drawn from Z. The second of these is the most interesting and I'll be spending longest on this."*

4 Lack of structure
Your audience will get lost if you don't give them a map of where you are going; for example: *"I've chosen three texts to analyse to illustrate my points, X, Y and Z. I'll use the first two to show how ... and the third to contrast that with ... After each text I'll summarise my points"*. It can be helpful to give some signposts along the way to show them where you have got to and where you will be going next; for example: *"So I've looked at this first text and shown how ... by giving examples of ... and now I'm going to ... before going on to ..."*.

5 Nothing to look at
It is hard just to listen to someone. It is easier when you have something to look at too. Provide your audience with handouts (containing a summary of your seminar, extracts from texts or crucial passages from your central sources). Use a whiteboard or blackboard to summarise your points or illustrate what you are talking about. Take flip-chart sheets which you have prepared beforehand to provide an overview, a map, a diagram. Use an overhead projector and prepare transparencies on each of your main points. Give your audience something to look at while you are talking.

6 Nothing to do

Just listening is dull. It is more interesting if the audience has something more active to do. This might involve reading a passage, analysing a text, solving a problem, suggesting alternative ways to interpret or analyse a passage or historical event, suggesting examples of a phenomenon or illustrations of a literary device or genre and so on. From time to time, give your audience some work to do.

7 Only note-taking

People won't join in, or even think very much, if they are furiously taking notes. Provide a handout so that your audience can concentrate on what you have to say.

8 No questions

If you talk non-stop, especially if you avoid eye contact with your audience, they are unlikely to ask you questions, even if they have questions in their minds. You need to invite questions. You can do this by saying at the start: *"Please stop me to ask questions or seek clarification."* You can stop and invite questions: *"Before I go on, is there anything you'd like to ask or for me to clarify?"*. You can stop and look round, inviting interruptions with your body language. Leave plenty of time even though the silence may feel threatening: it takes time to formulate questions. If none of these work, stop and ask people to write down two questions they would really like answered, give them a minute, and then take each person in turn and get them to read out their questions.

9 No questioning

Involve and challenge your audience by asking them questions. Prepare questions in advance. Don't ask "closed" questions, to which there is a right and wrong answer (*"Who wrote ...?" "Did ... write this before or after ...?"*) but open questions which can start a discussion (*"What might be the problems of this way of looking at things?" "Is this the only way of seeing this?" "What is your opinion on this?"*)

10 No summary

When you have finished, don't just suddenly stop and say: *"Well ... that's it really."* Summarise what you have said and make it clear what the key points were. Make sure your audience leave with a clear overview.

11 No discussion

Don't expect a discussion to happen all on its own. Make it clear you want some discussion: *"Let's stop for a few minutes to discuss this before I go on"*. Use body language to indicate that you are not about to start presenting again: sit down, relax, sit back, put your notes down. Think about what people might be interested in talking about and make suggestions: *"I thought it might be interesting to explore ... Do you think ... or ...?"* You can raise these issues at the start so that people are thinking about them while you are talking, and ready to join in when it is time to discuss.

12 Not drawing on what your audience know

People think more if they can relate what you are saying to what they know. Find out at the start what people have read and what they are familiar with and adjust your presentation accordingly. There is nothing more boring than going over ground everyone is already familiar with or dealing with something so outside everyone's experience that they can't relate to it. Half-way through ask: *"What else have people read which addresses these issues?"*

13 Reading out notes in full

Inexperienced presenters write out their presentation in full and read it out word for word. This is very dull for the audience and it isn't much fun for the presenter either. Experienced presenters rely on much briefer notes which give them an overview and a way of seeing very quickly what they are supposed to be talking about and what is coming next. Methods include:

- index cards which each contain one key idea or sub-section of the presentation;

- a handout for the audience which the presenter uses as a framework for the talk;

- transparencies which summarise the key points and which the presenter uses to remind herself;

- very brief skeleton notes containing only single words or phrases which provide clues about the content.

Your aim should be to be able to look up at your audience most of the time, and to give the impression of thinking while you are talking.

14 No follow-up

If the seminar is the last time anyone thinks about your topic, then no-one will learn much. Make suggestions about where your audience might read about your topic. Give references and suggest which ones are worth looking at and which parts are most interesting. Tell them where not to bother and what to avoid. Suggest what you'd have been interested to look at next if you'd had time.

15 No fun

Seminars don't have to be straight-faced and deadly serious. There will be more energy and involvement if people are enjoying themselves. Give yourself permission, and your audience permission, to relax and have a laugh.

16 No responsiveness or flexibility

Things don't always work out the way you thought. If you are way over people's heads or boring them to tears by going too fast, don't just plod on regardless. Stop and make sensible decisions about how to continue (*"What should I explain first if the rest of this is going to make sense to you?" "Would it be helpful if I stopped for a minute and let you catch up and ask some questions?"*).

17 No improvement

It is not possible to be brilliant at giving seminars first time. But you can learn and improve if you find out what went well and what could be changed. Ask your audience, or ask your tutor: *"What do you think I did well in my presentation and what would you suggest I improved for next time?"* Use this short questionnaire to get your audience to give you feedback.

Seminar Presentation Feedback Form

1 **Pace** too fast about right too slow
☐ ☐ ☐ ☐ ☐

2 **Quantity** too much about right too little
☐ ☐ ☐ ☐ ☐

3 **Clarity & structure** very clear adequate muddled
☐ ☐ ☐ ☐ ☐

4 **Interest** very interesting adequate dull
☐ ☐ ☐ ☐ ☐

5 **Notes & handouts** full and clear adequate poor none
☐ ☐ ☐ ☐ ☐

6 **Use of visual aids** very helpful adequate poor none
☐ ☐ ☐ ☐ ☐

7 **Discussion** very engaging adequate poor none
☐ ☐ ☐ ☐ ☐

8 **References** full and clear adequate poor none
☐ ☐ ☐ ☐ ☐

_____

Best features of the seminar

_____

Suggestions for improvement for your next seminar presentation

Involving Students in Discussion

Ground rules

Sometimes there are implicit "ground rules" operating in a group which obstruct its effective operation, for example: *It is acceptable to turn up late having done no reading, and to criticise and be rude to others.* No-one agreed these "rules", but the group operates as if they were there, just the same. It is possible to establish your own ground rules explicitly in a way which supports your group. You can discuss what you would like these ground rules to be. They might include:

- Don't interrupt people while they are speaking.
- Turn up on time.
- If you have to miss a meeting, let someone know in advance.
- Do at least some reading in preparation.
- If you have done no preparation at all, don't turn up.
- Seek consensus and common ground rather than confrontation.
- Don't dominate and overpower others.
- Actively encourage others to join in.
- If you want to criticise, criticise people's ideas rather than them personally.
- Be supportive and encourage each other.

Once you have agreed some ground rules you can write them up into a "charter" or "contract" and give everyone a copy. It can be worthwhile spending a few minutes every so often looking back at your ground rules and discussing whether you are keeping to them, and whether they need adjusting.

Rounds

Each person in the group in turn says something in relation to a theme; for example:

- *"My reaction to this text is ..."*
- *"One question I'd like an answer to is ..."*
- *"Something I've read in relation to this is ..."*

This is particularly useful to start a session as it gets everyone to say at least something and doesn't allow anyone to keep quiet. It is also useful at the end to summarise what people have got out of the session:

- *"Something I've learnt today is ..."*
- *"Something I'd like to do some follow-up reading on is ..."*

Individual work

Sometimes the reason no-one joins in is that they haven't got anything to say. If you give everyone a minute or two to read an extract, look through their notes or jot down outstanding questions they are then much more likely to have something they want to say.

Pairs

If your ideas haven't really formed clearly yet you may feel inhibited about saying them "in public". However, it would be easy in a pair. You can suggest that the members of the group spend five minutes in pairs discussing a topic, analysing a text or whatever before opening it out to the whole group.

5.2 Case study 2: Peer assessment of seminars in Education

This case study concerns an Education course in which classes of about 80 were commonly split into parallel seminar groups of eight to ten. After a session in which all 80 were together, the students split up into their groups in separate rooms and two members of each group were responsible for running the session. A single tutor toured the groups to check that everything was all right, sitting in on perhaps two sessions each week for about 20 minutes each.

What made the students take these sessions seriously was that peer-assessment of seminar presentations counted for 20% of the marks for the course. The criteria used are displayed in the handout below. Half the marks were for content and half for process, so students had to pay attention not just to their research beforehand, but to the way they would present the information and lead a discussion. This led to better-quality presentation and to more interesting discussions, which often took the form of role plays, simulations and debates. While students seem not to object to dull seminars run by tutors, they will not tolerate dull sessions run by their colleagues and this encouraged students to be imaginative and well prepared. The quality of the sessions was very high and the tutors were largely redundant, students almost resenting the tutor's intrusions, "their" seminars.

On some courses the students started the term with an exercise to discuss what made a good seminar and each group produced its own list of criteria which it used in assessment. What may have been lost in tutor control of this process was more than compensated for by students' sense of "owning" and running their own process.

Sets of criteria such as those below can be produced to affect any aspect of students' behaviour which you might want to change, such as the quality of their preparation.

Seminar Assessment Criteria

20% of the marks for the course are awarded for each of two seminar presentations, which you share with your seminar partner. These marks are awarded by the audience at each seminar. Please assess your colleagues' seminar presentations using this form. Think about each criterion separately and thoughtfully rather than giving one global snap judgement. Add comments explaining your marks under each criterion and some helpful comments at the end. Complete the form immediately at the end of the seminar and hand it in to your tutor.

Seminar presenters: 1 .... 2.................................

Criterion		Mark					
Content	clarity of argument, understanding, explanation, overview, conclusions. <u>Comments:</u>	0	1	2	3	4	5
Sources	breadth and relevance, acknowledgement of sources, references, reading list. <u>Comments:</u>	0	1	2	3	4	5
Presentation	voice, use of a.v. aids, pace, variety, liveliness, handouts. <u>Comments:</u>	0	1	2	3	4	5
Discussion	involvement of group, questioning, answering, use of discussion methods. <u>Comments:</u>	0	1	2	3	4	5

Best things about the seminar

What you should pay attention to next time

Total mark ☐

6 Making the most of infrequent discussion

As student numbers increase, one way of retaining seminar groups is to make them fortnightly, or even less frequent, rather than weekly. When seminars, tutorials and problem sessions are less frequent, a range of new problems become prominent:

- students do not get to know each other so well;

- the tutor does not get to know the students;

- everyone forgets what they were supposed to have prepared;

- any preparation may have been undertaken too long ago;

- for many issues, the moment has passed before the session comes along;

- continuity is broken and links are harder to make between sessions;

- sessions get out of sync with other elements on the course;

- momentum is lost and it is harder to get sessions rolling quickly;

- there is too much material to deal with, and too many questions to address, in too little time.

As a consequence of these problems there is a tendency for infrequent discussions to become unsatisfactory tutor monologues. Instead of sessions with tutors being considered precious and valuable they become devalued and poorly attended.

The diagrams below show how infrequent discussion meetings can be made central again, and more effective, by getting students to see them as part of a wider pattern of studying which they have to manage for themselves. The first three models shown assume that students will do preparatory work prior to discussion with their teacher, and follow-up and integrative work afterwards. In the fourth model the teacher briefs the students before they begin to work alone.

Such patterns of meetings can encourage student independence, but they are unlikely to establish such patterns on their own. Tutors will need to brief students clearly, explaining the purpose of the meetings, how they should be conducted and how they can be prevented from reverting to their old, unuseful form.

Infrequent discussion: patterns of meetings

These diagrams illustrate ways of organising group work so that students experience more discussion and are more prepared and purposeful when they meet their tutor, without increasing teaching hours.

When students meet without their tutor they can:

- prepare questions or reports;
- start to design, build, test or problem-solve;
- share independent reading, problems or calculations;
- analyse cases, data or specimens;
- review articles or chapters;
- brief each other on topics;
- answer each other's questions so that the tutor is asked only those questionsthat no-one can answer;
- carry out work set by the tutor;
- follow up ideas suggested by the tutor.

When students are with their tutor they can concentrate on:

- receiving feedback on work;
- asking outstanding questions;
- interrogating the tutor;
- receiving briefings for tasks;
- presenting the outcomes of work done beforehand;
- seeking inspiration.

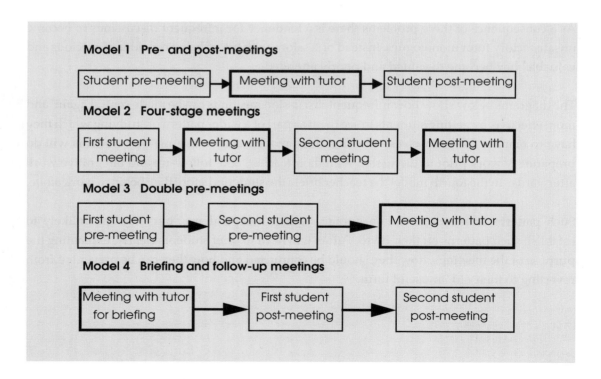

7 Action planning

Drawing on ideas elsewhere in this booklet, put together outline plans for protecting and improving student discussion on your course, even though you have more students.

How could discussion meetings be organised? (Size, frequency, tutor involvement)

How could these meetings be run differently to enhance the quality of discussion?

What support would students (or tutors) need to implement this new system?

What would it cost in terms of teaching hours, compared with your existing system?

What would you have to do to put these plans into action?

Who or what could support you?

Who or what could stop you, and how could you overcome these blocks?

Bibliography

Bligh, D. (1986), <u>Teach Thinking by Discussion</u>. Guildford: Society for Research in Higher Education.

Collier, G. (1983), <u>The Management of Peer-Group Learning: Syndicate Methods in Higher Education.</u> Guildford: Society for Research in Higher Education.

Cryer, P. & Elton, L. (1992), <u>Promoting Active Learning in Large Classes.</u> Sheffield Universities Staff Development and Training Unit

Frederick, J. (1987), "Student Involvement: Active Learning in Large Classes." In M.G. Weimer (Ed.) <u>Teaching Large Classes Well</u>. London: Jossey-Bass.

Gibbs, G., Habeshaw, S., & Habeshaw, T. (1992),   <u>53 Interesting Ways To Teach Large Classes.</u> Bristol: Technical and Educational Services.

Goodlad, S. (1989), <u>Peer Tutoring.</u> London: Kogan Page.

Habeshaw, S., Habeshaw, T. & Gibbs, G. (1989), <u>53 Interesting Things To Do In Your Seminars and Tutorials</u>. Bristol: Technical and Educational Services.

Jaques, D. (1991), <u>Learning in Groups.</u> London: Kogan Page.

Jenkins, A. & Gibbs, G. (1992), <u>Teaching Large Classes.</u> London: Kogan Page.

Jenkins, A. & Pepper, D. (1989), <u>Enhancing Employability and Educational Experience: Developing Communication and Group Work Skills.</u> Birmingham: Standing Conference on Educational Development.

Magin, D., Nightingale, P., Andresen, L. & Boud, D. (1989), <u>Strategies for Increasing Students' Independence.</u> Teaching with Reduced Resources, no. 2. Kensington: Professional Development Centre. University of New South Wales.

Michaelson, L.K. (1983), "Team Learning in Large Classes." In C. Bouton and R.Y .Garth (Eds.) <u>Learning in Groups</u>. London: Jossey-Bass.

Weaver, R.L. (1983), "Small Group Teaching in Large Classes", <u>Educational Forum</u>, 48 (1), 65-73.